JOHANN SEBASTIAN BACH

SELECTED WORKS
FOR ORGAN

Edited by

EDOUARD NIES-BERGER
CHARLES-MARIE WIDOR

and

ALBERT SCHWEITZER

G. SCHIRMER, Inc.

DISTRIBUTED BY
HAL•LEONARD®
CORPORATION
7777 W. BLUEMOUND RD. P.O. BOX 13819 MILWAUKEE, WI 53213

Ed. 3486

CONTENTS

Prepare { U Bb ⑩ 00 7717 112
P 64

Prelude and Fugue in C Major

Prelude and Fugue in G Minor

Fugue

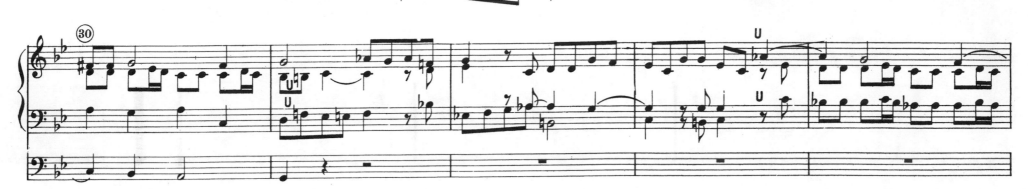

Prepare {
U Bb ⑩ 00 7848 346
L Bb ⑩ 00 7888 567
P 64
}

Prelude and Fugue in A Minor

Prelude

Manual

Pedal

Fugue

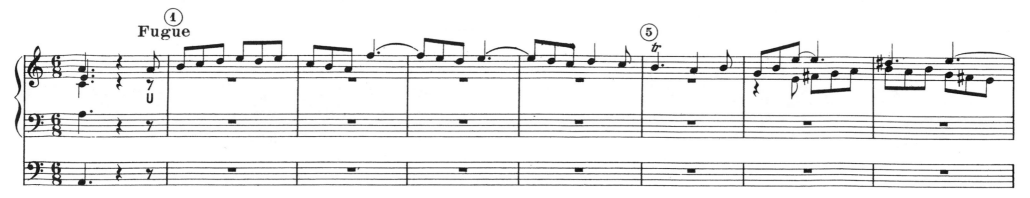

Sonata II

a 2 Clav.

e

Pedale

Largo

Allegro

48624

Herzlich thut mich verlangen

1. Wachet auf, ruft uns die Stimme

Canto fermo in Tenore

48624

In dulci jubilo

Manuale

Pedale

Liebster Jesu, wir sind hier

distinctius
In Canone alla Quinta

Manuale

Pedale

Blank pages in the manuscript.

48624

Jesu, meine Freude

Manuale

Pedale

Doric Toccata and Fugue

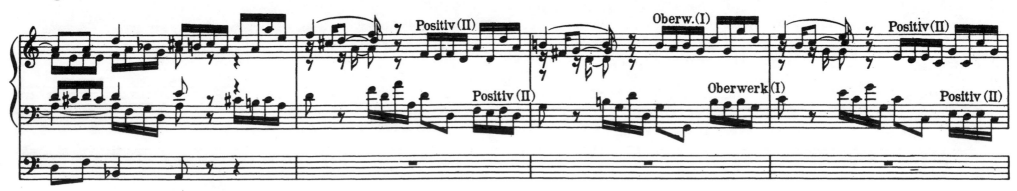

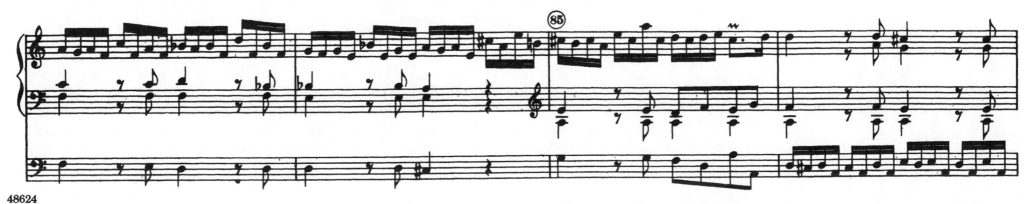

Fuge

Canzona in D Minor

Manual

Pedal

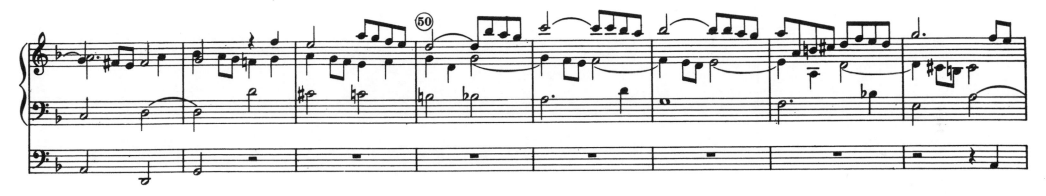

Pastorale in F Major

Manual

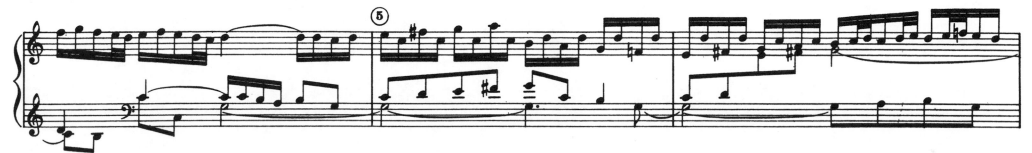

Manual

Prelude and Fugue in E♭ Major

(St. Anne's)

48624

Fugue

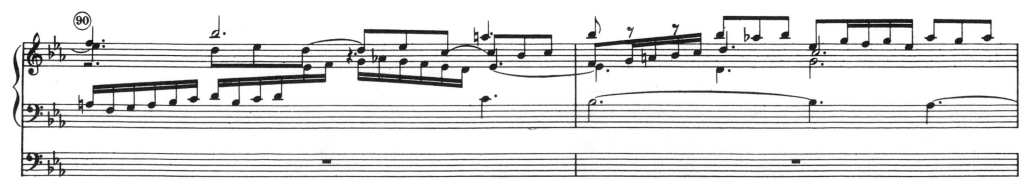

Prelude and Fugue in G Minor
(The Great)

Prelude (Fantasia)

Fugue

48624

Prelude and Fugue in E Minor

(The Cathedral)

Fugue

Toccata and Fugue in D Minor

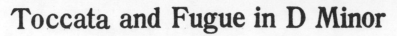

Fugue

Presto

135

Adagio Vivace

140

Molto adagio

Passacaglia and Thema Fugatum in C minor

Thema fugatum